CW00868208

Make and Play
AEROPLANES

Written by David Holzer
Illustrated by Maureen Galvani

TOP THAT! Kids™

Published by Top That! Publishing plc
Tide Mill Way, Woodbridge, Suffolk, IP12 1AP, UK
www.topthatpublishing.com

The Story of Flight

Ever since human beings first looked up at the sky and saw birds flying they wondered how it would be possible for humans to do the same. Today, people fly on aeroplanes all the time but do you ever think about how they fly?

Leonardo da Vinci

You might have heard of a man called Leonardo da Vinci who lived in the fifteenth century. Did you know that he was an amazing inventor who drew flying machines, inspired by watching birds?

When humans took to the sky, the machines they flew were very like Leonardo's drawings.

Leonardo's flying machine.

Orville and Wilbur Wright

At Kitty Hawk, North Carolina, in the USA, on 17th December, 1903, two brothers, Orville and Wilbur Wright, flew a motor-driven aeroplane operated by a human being for the first time.

The Wright brother's aeroplane *Flyer*.

This book will explain how aeroplanes fly, show you how to make your own model planes and teach you about flying. There's also a cool Barnstormer for you to make that comes with this book.

Today, planes can fly at twice the speed of sound (imagine that!), many miles above Earth's surface. Manned space-craft regularly go to the moon and unmanned spacecraft travel millions of miles into space.

How Aeroplanes Fly

Have you ever looked up at a passing aeroplane and asked yourself how it stays up there? How can something fly if it is very heavy? It is not as complicated as you might think.

A simple way to understand how an aeroplane stays up in the air is to look at something called Bernoulli's Principle. Before we learn about that though, we need to see how the plane gets up in the air in the first place.

Thrust

If you have flown on an aeroplane, you will have felt the amazing power in the engines used to fly the plane. The power generated by the engines is called 'thrust'. Engines have to be powerful because they need to provide enough thrust to help lift enormous aircraft and their passengers.

A jumbo jet can carry nearly 500 people. Think how heavy that is! Or try to imagine the thrust needed to lift the Boeing 777-30, the world's longest commercial jet airliner.

When pilots fly aeroplanes they have to control the amount of thrust at different times during the flight.

Lots of power is needed to get the plane off the ground and into the air but once it is up, less is needed and the pilot has to make sure that the engines provide enough power to help keep the plane at the right speed to stay up in the air.

When the aeroplane is landing, the pilot needs to use the engines and the 'ailerons' – flaps on the wings – to slow the plane down so it lands safely. He does this by reducing power but also by moving the ailerons down so that they create more 'drag' or become more difficult to move through the air.

Bernoulli's Principle

Daniel Bernoulli was an eighteenth-century scientist from Switzerland. Bernoulli's Principle explains the reason why an aeroplane's wings are shaped the way they are. If you look at an aeroplane's wing, you will see that the bottom is flat and the top is curved.

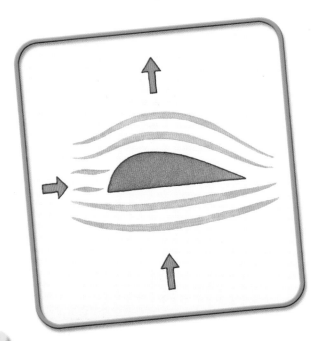

When the aeroplane is flying, air moves more slowly over the bottom of the wing than it does over the top. The slower-moving air creates more pressure than the air flowing over the top of the wing. As there is more pressure being applied upwards than downwards, the plane stays up in the air.

Racing Cars and Aerofoils

Racing cars also use aerofoils that operate in the opposite way. As racing cars go so fast, they could take off! Aerofoils are used to make the cars heavy enough for them to stay on the ground.

Make Your Own Wing

To see how wings and aerofoils use the air that flows over and under their wings to lift off and stay up, try these simple experiments? They will show how gravity and air pressure work.

Experiment 1

1 Place one end of the strip of paper between the pages of the book so that the other end hangs over the top.

2 Move the book quickly through the air or blow across the top of the piece of paper – it should move upwards.

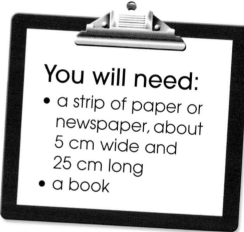

You will need:
- a strip of paper or newspaper, about 5 cm wide and 25 cm long
- a book

Experiment 2

1 Hold the two sheets of paper about 10 cm apart.

2 Blow between them.

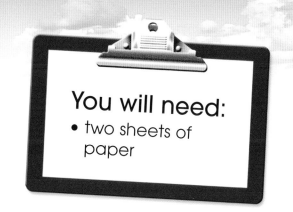

You will need:
- two sheets of paper

Instead of flying apart, the two sheets of paper should have moved together. This is because the air moving quickly between the two pieces of paper has less pressure than the air pressing on the outsides of the paper.

Experiment 3

Ask an adult to help you with this experiment.

If you don't have a vacuum cleaner like this in your house, ask an adult if they know someone who has one.

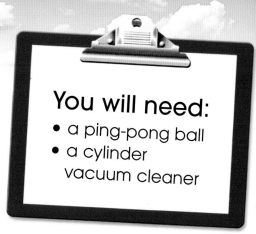

You will need:
- a ping-pong ball
- a cylinder vacuum cleaner

1 Connect the hose to the blower, not to the suction end, of the vacuum cleaner.

2 Turn the switch on.

3 Hold the hose/nozzle vertically so that the stream of air is going straight up.

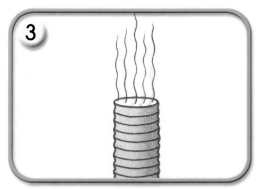

4 Let go of the ping-pong ball into the stream of air, about 30 cm away from the nozzle.

5 Slowly tip the nozzle so that the air shoots up at an angle – the ball will stay suspended in the stream of air.

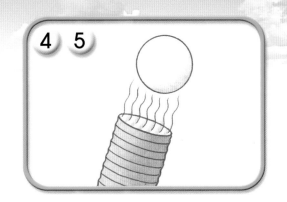

How it works
1 The force of gravity acting on the ball means that it wants to fall out of the air stream.
2 The fast moving air lessens the air pressure on the part of the ball still in the air stream.
3 This overcomes the force of gravity, which leaves the ball suspended.

The Parts of an Aeroplane

Although aeroplanes come in many different sizes depending on what their job is, they use the same parts to take off and fly.

This diagram shows you the main parts of an aeroplane.

Wings
Generate lift

Jet Engine
Generates thrust

Cockpit
Command and control

Fuselage (Body)
Holds things together
(Carries payload – fue

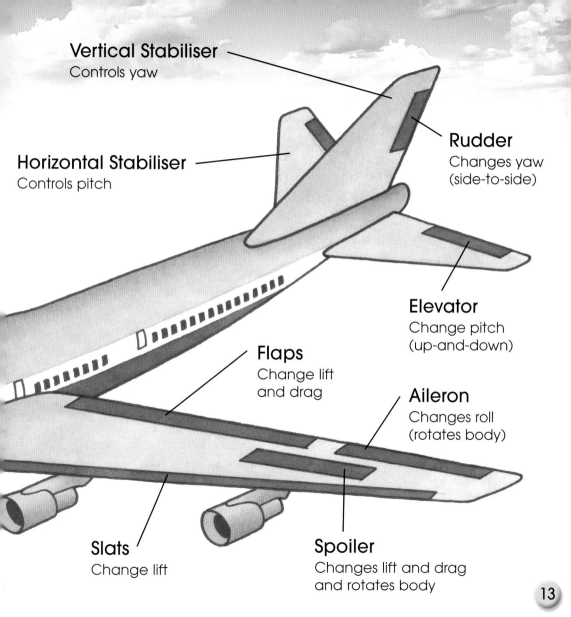

Vertical Stabiliser
Controls yaw

Horizontal Stabiliser
Controls pitch

Rudder
Changes yaw
(side-to-side)

Elevator
Change pitch
(up-and-down)

Flaps
Change lift
and drag

Aileron
Changes roll
(rotates body)

Slats
Change lift

Spoiler
Changes lift and drag
and rotates body

13

The wings generate most of the lift that holds the plane in the air and lift is made by the thrust from the engines usually found beneath the wings.

At the back of the aeroplane is the tail – made up of a fixed horizontal piece and a fixed vertical piece. The vertical piece keeps the plane's nose from swinging from side to side and the horizontal piece stops it moving up and down.

On the back of the wings and tail pieces are small moving sections attached to the fixed sections by hinges. The piece at the back of the vertical part of the tail is called the rudder and it steers the tail from the left to the right. The 'elevator' on the horizontal piece moves the tail up and down.

The outward hinged part of a wing is called the 'aileron' and it rolls the wings from side to side. There are also 'flaps', hinged sections near the plane's body that are moved downwards on takeoff and landing.

Playing with Propellers

Propellers actually exist in nature. If you have ever picked up a sycamore seed, you will have found a simple natural propeller. The long part of the seed sends it spinning through the air.

Watching natural propellers may have given Leonardo da Vinci – who, as we know, invented many different kinds of flying machine – the idea for his 'aerial screw', the ancestor of the modern propeller. Leonardo's invention used a flat screw that would create lift when it was turned. Now, we have helicopters like the Apache that can fly as fast as 260 km/h.

An Apache helicopter.

How a Propeller Works

A propeller is like a spinning wing that, instead of pushing air behind a plane to lift it upwards, pulls in air to move a helicopter upwards and forwards. Propellers are shaped like aerofoils.

The amount of thrust created by a propeller depends on how fast, and at what angle, its blades cut through the air.

Propellers are used not just in helicopters and aeroplanes but to power hovercraft and submarines and also to keep huge engines cool.

Make Your Own Propeller

Propellers can have between two and four blades. You can make your own two-bladed propeller by following these instructions:

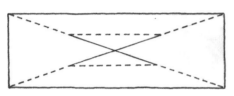

1 Copy this diagram onto the card.

2 Cut along the dotted lines carefully.

3 Slowly push a pencil point. through the centre of the card and turn the pencil as you go.

You will need:
- a piece of card 9 cm x 3 cm
- a drinking straw

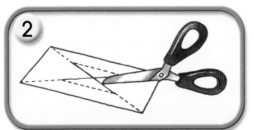

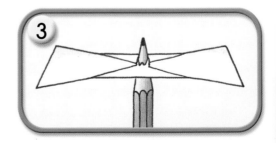

4 Make the hole just big enough for you to put the straw through.

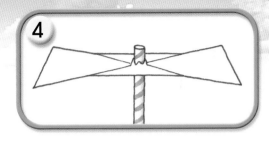

5 Bend the blades at an angle.

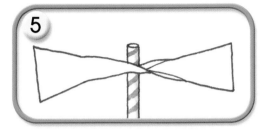

When you spin the straw between your fingers you will feel a breeze. Colour the blades of your propeller and you can make it look like one of the toy windmills you get at the seaside.

Today, wind farms use their propeller blades to turn wind power into electricity without making pollution.

How Thrust Works

The way balloons that carry people work is really simple. Two Frenchmen, the Montgolfier brothers, were sitting around a fire some time in 1783 wondering what makes smoke rise. "Perhaps warm air is lighter than cold air and this makes it go up," one said. They soon found out that this was true.

This discovery was actually the beginning of attempts to make an aircraft powerful enough to carry people.

Big balloons are powered by a fire that blows hot air up into the mouth of the balloon. The height of the balloon is controlled by adjusting the amount of hot air allowed into the balloon.

This is why they are called hot-air balloons.

Making Your Own Balloon Rocket

You can make a balloon rocket really easily by blowing it up, stretching the neck wide apart, using two hands, and letting go.

First Rubber Balloons

Professor Michael Faraday, a famous inventor, made the first rubber balloons in 1824. He used them in experiments with hydrogen.

Greatest Distance flown in a Hot Air Balloon

The greatest distance travelled in a manned balloon is 40,815 km, made by Bertrand Piccard and Brian Jones, in 1999.

The Highest Hot-air Balloon Flight

On 6th June, 1988, Per Lindstrand achieved the altitude record of 19,811 m in a Colt 600 hot-air balloon over Laredo, Texas, USA.

Create Your Own Thrust

It's good fun to make a balloon rocket and have a race with your friends.
Ask an adult to help you.

Race 1

1 Blow up the balloons and pinch the necks so air doesn't escape.

2 Place your balloons lengthwise on the polystyrene trays.

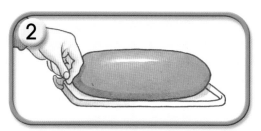

3 Put a piece of tape over each balloon and stick each end to the tray.

4 Put the balloons and trays on the water and let go.

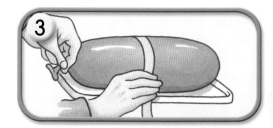

Race 2

1 Pull a piece of string taut through each of the straws tying each end to chairs.

2 Blow up your balloons, holding the neck so the air won't escape.

3 Tape the straws holding the string to the balloons.

4 Let go of the balloons and see which team's moves along the string the fastest.

How it works

Your balloons are powered by the air that has been compressed inside the balloon rushing out through the neck. The air is the thrust.

Make Your Own Bottle Flyer

This model plane can be made from an empty fizzy drink bottle in no time at all!

You will need:
- an empty fizzy drink bottle that still has its cap
- plenty of thin card
- pens, sticky putty and double-sided tape, which comes with this book
- a ruler
- an adult to help you

1 Copy the shapes and measurements of these diagrams onto the card.

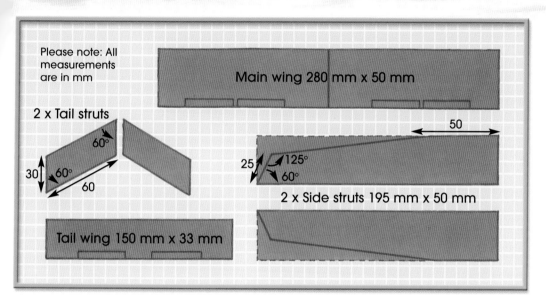

Please note: All measurements are in mm

2 x Tail struts

Main wing 280 mm x 50 mm

60°

30 60°

60

50

25 125°

60°

2 x Side struts 195 mm x 50 mm

Tail wing 150 mm x 33 mm

2 Stick the tail struts to the side struts using double-sided sticky tape.

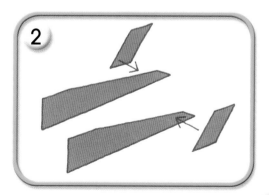

2

3 Use sticky tape to join the assembled tail struts and side struts to the bottle.

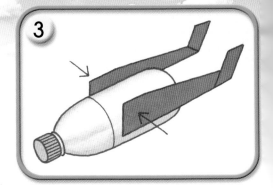

4 Tape the main wing to the bottle so that it's supported by the side struts and use scissors to create even sections of trim.

5 Use sticky tape to stick the tail wing on top of the tail struts.

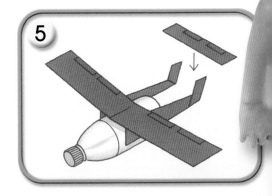

6 Put a small ball of sticky putty on the cap.

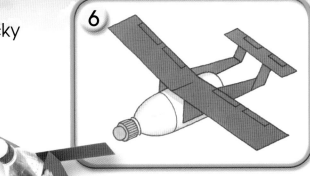

Now your plane is ready to fly. The best way to launch it is at shoulder height. Why don't you ask your brother, sister or a friend to make a bottle flyer as well so that you can have races?

What is a Barnstormer?

Back in the early days of flying, after WW1 ended in 1918, men who used to be pilots in the Air Force flew around America in ex-Air Force planes giving death-defying, breath-taking demonstrations of stunt flying.

These fearless pilots were called barnstormers because, when they flew into town to give a demonstration, they usually landed at a farm. Farms had plenty of big fields for them to land on. They would start by flying low over the farm's barns.

As well as performing in small towns, barnstormers did stunts at air shows and in front of Hollywood movie cameras.

Barnstorming stunts

Barnstormers did everything with their planes that you could possibly think of. Pilots looped-the-loop and did barrel roll moves. Other pilots walked, or even danced, on the wings of their planes, played tennis between planes, climbed from plane to plane and practised shooting at targets.

A brave barnstormer performs a stunt.

A classic barnstorming stunt.

A model based on a classic barnstorming plane is included with this book. Turn the page and find out how to make your own plane.

Build a Barnstormer

Ask an adult to help you make this model.

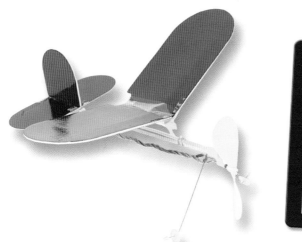

You will need:
- the barnstormer pieces from the kit with this book

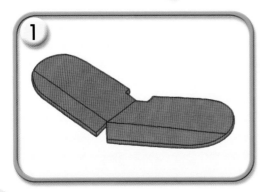

1 Gently bend along the centre and horizontal scored lines of the wings.

2 Attach the wing support to the main wing using the two sections of tape marked W-1 on the yellow sheet of paper.

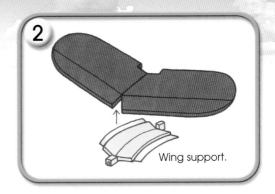

Wing support.

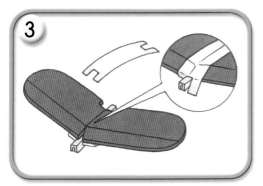

3 Use the H-shaped piece of tape marked W-2 to secure the wing support to the main wings from above.

4 Connect the tail fin to the tail plane then slot the whole thing into the tail support. Secure it in place using the pieces of tape marked W-3.

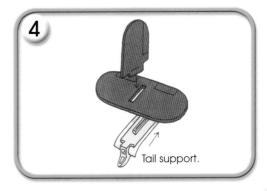

Tail support.

5 Attach the plastic component marked 'A' to the wooden bar by wrapping an elastic band around each plastic notch, then under the bar and back over the notch to secure. Join the wing support to the component marked 'A' and the tail plane to one end of the wooden bar.

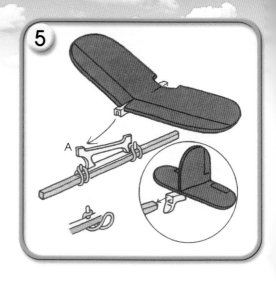

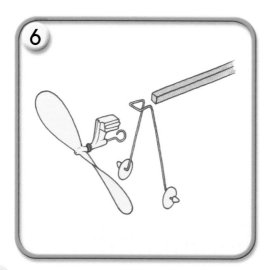

6 Attach the front wheels by allowing the metal notch to overlap the spare end of the wooden bar. Push the propeller section over the end to secure it.

7 Thread the thick elastic band through the notch on the tail support. Pull the band through its own loop. Secure to the wire hook on the propeller section.

When you've made the barnstormer and you're ready to fly it, all you need to do is spin the propeller to tighten the elastic band and throw it gently up into the air.

Cool Concorde

Concorde was one of the fastest and most beautiful planes that ever flew. Here are some fascinating facts and figures about this remarkable plane.

The first commercial flight of Concorde took place in 1969. Its first round the world flight took place on 8th November, 1986 and it covered 45,444 km in 29 hours 59 minutes.

Concorde was 62 m long and stretched between 15–25 cm in flight because the frame heated up. Its wingspan was 230 cm. This is less than an ordinary aircraft because Concorde used 'vortex lift' to fly.

Concorde's nose could be lowered on take-off and landing so that the pilots could see where they are going.

A typical London to New York crossing on Concorde used to take less than three-and-a-half hours and, because Concorde was travelling westwards, it actually arrived before it left.

Concorde cruised at more than twice the speed of sound, over 17 km above sea level. Each of Concorde's four engines gave more than 18.7 tonnes of thrust burning a total 25,629 litres of fuel and, when the plane was flying, they were the most powerful, pure jet engines flying.

More than 2.5 million passengers flew on Concorde between the time it began flying in 1976 and when it stopped in 2003. The most frequent passenger flew on Concorde nearly 70 times every year.

Make Your Own Concorde

It's easy to make your own streamlined model of probably the most famous aeroplane in the world if you follow these simple instructions. Then you can have fun seeing how far you can get your Concorde to fly.

You will need:
- thin card
- sticky tape
- scissors

1 Cut out a piece of thin card that's 410 mm long and 140 mm wide. Roll it into a tube so that it's still 410 mm long but 45 mm in diameter. Use sticky tape to hold the card in place at each end.

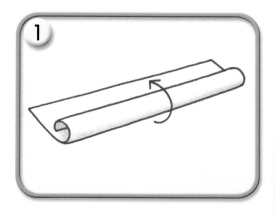

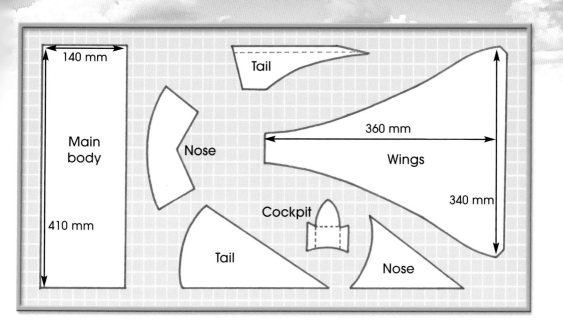

140 mm

Main body

410 mm

Tail

Nose

Tail

Cockpit

360 mm

Wings

340 mm

Nose

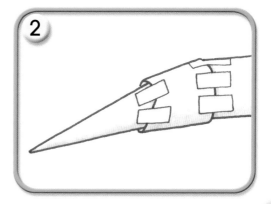

2 Cut out the two nose cone pieces from the card. Tape them to the body, as shown.

3 Copy the wings shape and cut it out of a piece of thin card. It should be 360 mm x 340 mm.

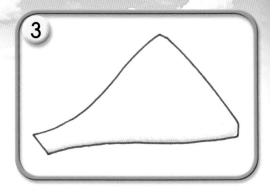

4 Tape the wings to the top of the body, as shown. Cut out the cockpit and attach to the top of the nose, as shown.

5 Cut the tail sections out of another piece of card. Stick the pieces to the Concorde with sticky tape.

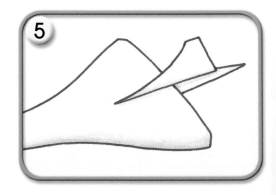

6 Use your pens to decorate the model. How will you decorate yours?

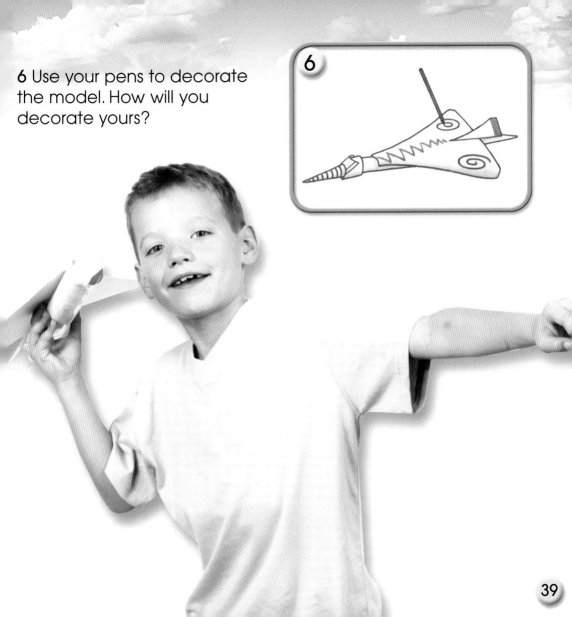

Fighter Planes

The first fighter planes, made out of wood, wire and fabric, took to the skies when WW1 broke out in 1914. Today, military aeroplanes can fly at up to three times the speed of sound.

Aeroplanes flown during WW1 weren't actually powerful enough to carry guns because the vibration would have thrown them off target. However, as the war went on, aeroplanes became more powerful and the pilots fought battles in the sky called dogfights.

The German Fockewulf fighter plane.

The American P-51 Mustang fighter plane.

By WW2, fighter planes played a very important part in the fighting. The Battle of Britain, in 1940, was won by British pilots flying Hawk Hurricane and Spitfire fighter planes.

In 1944, the first jet fighter planes were developed and by the end of the war in 1945, they were flying in the air forces of most of the countries which were fighting.

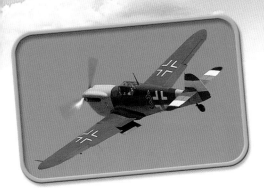

The German Messerschmitt.

Modern fighter planes are a vital part of any country's armed forces. Fighters like the Lockheed F-117 stealth fighters are able to intercept enemy planes and deliver powerful and sophisticated weapons to even the smallest of targets.

Today, the latest spy planes, controlled by computers, no longer have any need for a pilot!

Making a Paper Aeroplane

Making paper aeroplanes is great fun and, once you've learned the basics, you can go on to make planes that are more difficult to design. You could even create your own designs.

1 Start by finding a flat surface – like a table – to work on.

2 First, fold the piece of paper in half the long way, like this.

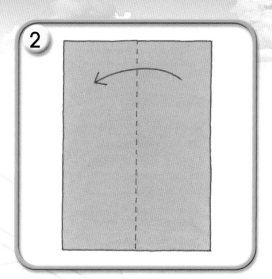

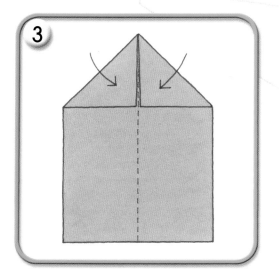

3 Next, open it out and fold the top corners in and down like this.

4 Then fold the top `triangle' down like this.

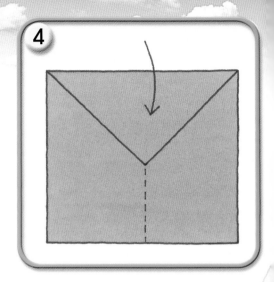

5 Now fold the top corners down again, as before.

6 Fold the paper in half lengthways again.

7 Fold the wings down like this.

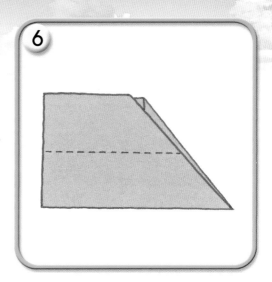

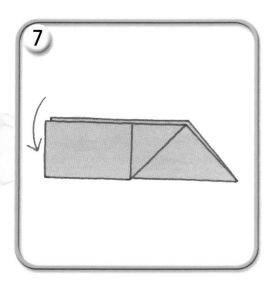

Top Tip!
Why not use some scissors to create ailerons and flaps? You can see for yourself the effects they have on your aeroplane.

8 Finally, fold the tips of the wings up like this. Now you're ready to soar!

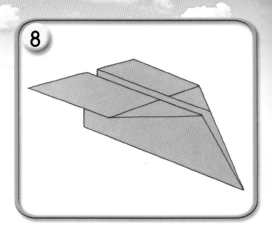

Your plane is now finished and ready to fly. When you want to fly it, hold it along the central fold, pointing slightly upwards. You might want to experiment with sliding a paper clip along the nose of the plane to see how this helps it fly.

You can also decorate your plane using the felt pens that come with this book. Always remember not to aim your paper plane at other people or at animals.

Have fun
flying your plane.

Fantastic Facts

Here are some facts about aircraft and the wonderful world of flight that will amaze and astound you.

Convertiplanes can hover like helicopters and convert into winged aeroplanes for flying forward.

In 2002, a hypersonic jet engine flew at over seven times the speed of sound over the Australian desert.

On board the Lear Jet 35, passengers can use the internet, email and telephone.

The 'Spruce Goose' was the largest aircraft ever built and flew only once, in 1947.

The British Red Arrows stunt team often fly as low as 30 m above ground.

Acknowledgements

Key: Top - t; middle - m; bottom - b; left - l; right - r. Aviation Picture Library - APL.

2: APL. 3: (tr) NASA; (ml) Top That! 4: Corel. 7: Topham Picturepoint. 9: Top That!
11: Top That! 16: (tr) Top That!17: (tl) Corel; (b) Topham Picturepoint.
19: Topham Picturepoint. 20: Topham Picturepoint. 21-27: Top That!
28: Vince Streano/Corbis. 29: (mr) Bettmann/Corbis. 33: Top That!
34: Topham Picturepoint. 35: Corel. 39: Top That! 40: (bl) NASA; (mr) APL.
41: (tl) APL; (mr) Corel. 47: Top That! 48: Topham Picturepoint.